To my parents and step-parents

Joan & Rusty Little ♥ Bob & Charlene Carrick

My angels of support
and unconditional love.

The Odd Ones

By Wendy Fedan

At the edge of a stream
lived a group of little turtles.
They were peaceful,
shy creatures
~ that is, all but one ~
the smallest turtle in the bunch.
His name was Tuffy.

One day, as the turtles lay sunning
themselves on the bank of the bubbling
stream, a fox wandered over.
The fox thought the little turtles were
pebbles, so he took no notice
and bent down to drink.

Tuffy poked his little head
out of his shell and snapped,
"Get out of our water!
This is our place!"

"I've never heard a pebble talk,"
said the fox.

"Get back in your shell."
The other turtles pleaded.
"You'll get hurt!"

But Tuffy didn't listen.

He waddled up to the fox,
his head stretched high.
"Get out of our stream,
or I'll... I'll..." He thought hard.
"I'll bite your nose off!"

Annoyed with this talking pebble,
the fox lifted his front paw
and swatted little Tuffy away.

Tuffy
tumbled
across the
bank
and
CRASHED
into
the
other
turtles!

For a moment they were all flying, and then...

... SPLASH!

They landed in the stream.

Tuffy was surounded by cranky, wet turtles.

As the others struggled back on their feet, the largest turtle yelled at him.

"Next time you should think before coming out of your shell! For such a little turtle, you sure have a big mouth!"

Tuffy was embarrassed,
and wandered away into the woods.

When he was far away from the stream,
he stopped. Tuffy was lost and alone.

The small turtle sat down
and began to cry.

Tuffy stopped crying
when he heard a rustle of leaves
from somewhere in the dark woods.
The noise grew louder and louder.
Something big must be coming,
he thought. Another fox, perhaps?
Tuffy raised his head high,
ready to confront the stranger.

Suddenly a little mouse popped out from the bushes. The mouse ran to Tuffy, squeaking,

"Help me!
Oh, please help me,
little turtle!"

A big cat burst from the bushes
and the frightened little mouse
scurried behind the turtle.
Tuffy stood bravely to guard
the mouse, and the hungry
animal reached out with its claws
to swat Tuffy away.

Tuffy would not
be swatted this time.

He snapped at the paw, and
chomped the cat's big toe.
The cat screeched with pain
and scampered back
into the bushes!

"Oh, thank you!"
The mouse squeaked.

Tuffy introduced himself. "My name is Tuffy and I'm looking for a new home."

"Why?" Asked the mouse.

Tuffy sighed. "The other turtles don't want me around anymore."

"I know how you feel," squeaked the little mouse. "The mice back home make fun of me. They scurry around making nests, collecting food for winter. All I want to do is learn about the forest. There is so much the forest can teach us. Did you know butterflies used to be worms with legs?"

"No," Tuffy blinked.

"My name's Pitter," the mouse said.

Tuffy grinned happily, knowing he found a friend.

"Glad to meet you, Pitter."
Tuffy smiled.
"Since you know so much
about the forest,
could you help me search
for a new home?"

Pitter's eyes opened wide.
"I'll go with you! The birds told
me about a river not far away.
There we'll find tall grass and
deep water."

Are there rocks to lie on?"

"Oh, yes. Lots of them."

"Then let's go!"
Tuffy grinned.

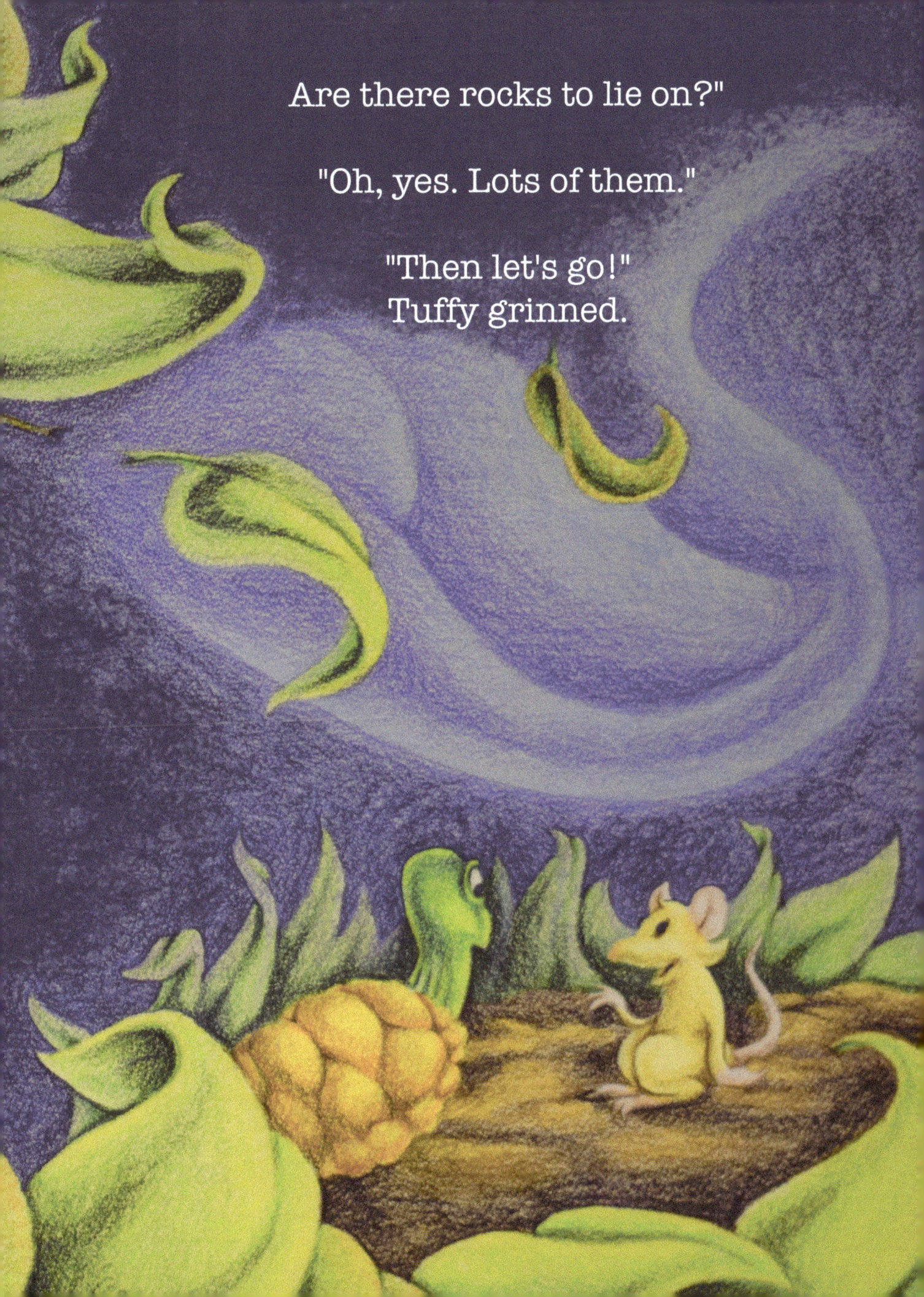

Tuffy was a slow traveler, but Pitter didn't mind.

She would stop to sniff wild flowers as she waited for her turtle friend to catch up.

After a long time,
Tuffy began to wonder
if they were lost,
but Pitter said the
river wasn't
much farther.

Finally they could see light behind
the forest trees. Their legs moved
faster with every step, until finally
they reached the edge of the woods.

Tuffy stared down at the huge river
in front of them.

"Wow!" Tuffy said.
He had never seen
so much water.

"Wow!" Pitter gasped,
looking down at the high grass
by the riverbank.

"Race you down there!"
She squeaked,
and scampered down the hill
into the grass below.

Tuffy knew he couldn't run like Pitter.
Instead he pulled his head and feet into his shell.
With a push and a wiggle, he was tumbling down
the hill so fast he passed little Pitter on the way!

Out of control, the turtle
rolled all the way to the
river's edge. He landed
with a splash among the lily
pads and sent a cluster
of frogs flying into the air!

Pitter scurried to the riverbank and found
poor Tuffy lying on his back in the water.
The frogs all jumped out of sight
behind some reeds.
That is, all but one.
"Are you all right, little turtle?"
Asked the frog with a tail.

"Oh, yes." Tuffy could see the other frogs
frowning at him from behind the reeds.
"I'm so sorry for the mess I've made.
I was hoping to find a new home here."

Before Tuffy could say another word,
some frogs leapt from the reeds
and began to shout.
"You can't live here,
you clumsy turtle!
Go back where you came from!"

The frog with the tail spoke gently to them.
"He said he was sorry. We should let him stay."

The other frogs were too angry to listen.
"Maybe you should go away with this strange
little turtle."
The mean frogs laughed and chanted,
"Polly, Polly, silly little froggy!
Wags her tail just like a doggie!"

Polly sniffed, trying to hide her tears. "They're always teasing me about my tail,"

"What's wrong with having a tail?" Tuffy asked.

Pitter tried to explain. "Remember when I told you a butterfly used to be a worm with legs? Well, a frog is like a butterfly -- only instead of growing wings, a baby tadpole loses its tail to become a frog."

"I never lost my tail," Polly sobbed.

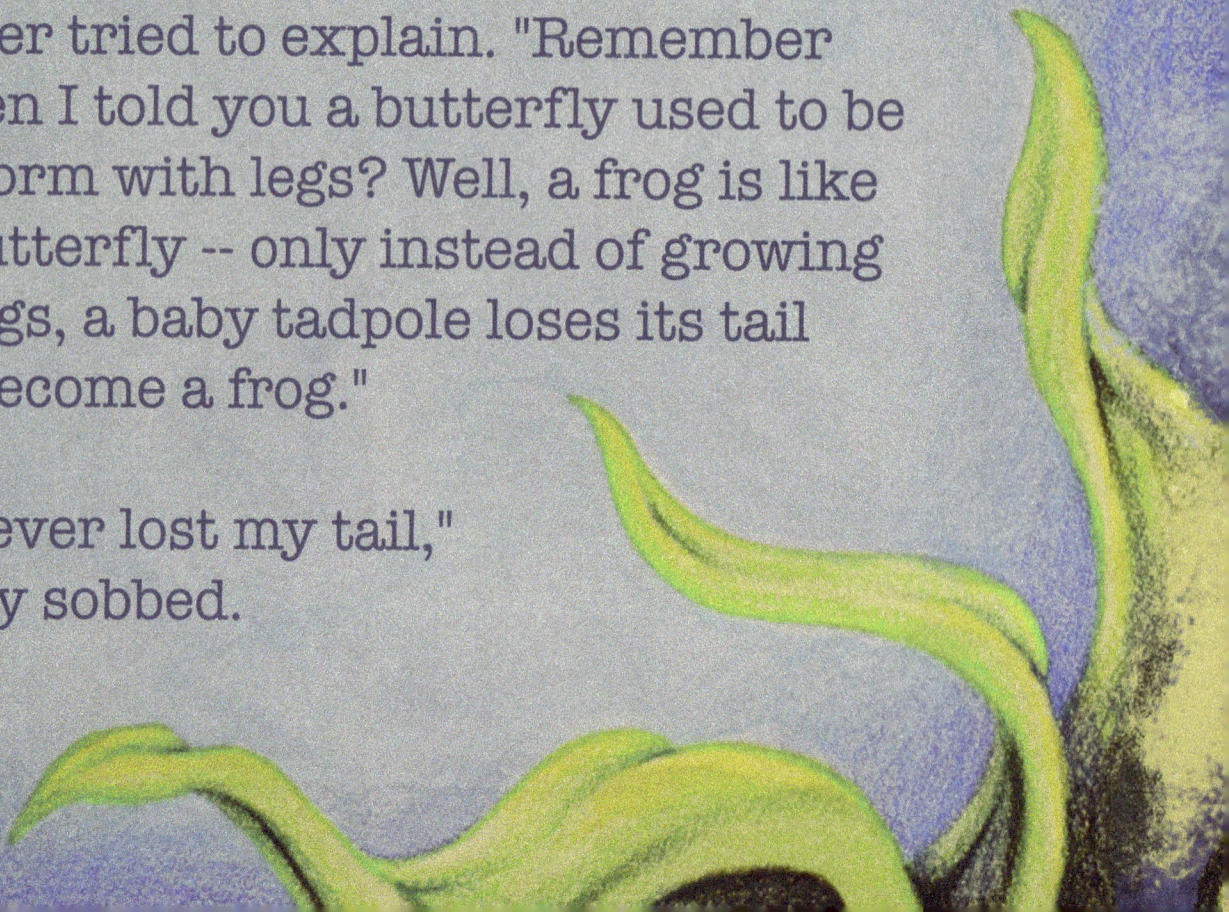

"Is that why the others tease you?" Tuffy asked.
The little frog nodded.

"Well, Polly," the mouse asked, "would you like to join us? We're looking for a home where we can be ourselves. A place where no one will tease us."

The frog smiled through her tears.
"That sounds wonderful!"

So the three small animals set off to cross the river, to live on the other side.

Polly and Tuffy were used to the water, but Pitter was afraid. She even shook when she thought of stepping into a puddle. A puddle was like a bath to a mouse.

Pitter rode Tuffy's back, gripping his shell tightly, and Polly led the way to the other side. Everything was fine until they were almost all the way across the river

Polly felt they were being followed. She turned around to look, and saw a big hungry fish with a mouth so huge it could eat all three of them in one gulp!

The mouse looked around, too. She saw the fish under the water, with its mouth open wide, ready for dinner.

The little mouse gasped,
"It's going to eat us!
It's going to eat us!"

"What? Where?" Tuffy wobbled, tipped over and Pitter fell with a splash!

Polly knew she had to do
something fast to save her friends.

The frog used her tadpole tail to steer herself and move quickly. She swam in circles around the fish, and made it dizzy.

"Eek! Eek!" Pitter squeaked, as Tuffy bit at her ears to keep her above water.

Mouth full, Tuffy mumbled, "Climb on!" Pitter scrambled up on his shell and squeezed the turtle's neck to hang on tight.

Tuffy paddled
as fast as he could
with the sopping
wet mouse
on his back.

Pitter looked
back to the river.
She could not see
Polly.

"Polly!"
She called.

"Pol-l-leee!"
Tuffy hollered.

Tuffy's eyes filled with tears
as he thought about the brave little
frog who risked her life
to save them.

Suddenly, Pitter gave a little squeak and pointed to the water. Tuffy looked and saw something swimming towards them.

They laughed when they saw it was Polly!

When Polly reached
the riverbank, the others
called her a hero.

"You're a hero, too, Tuffy."
Pitter said. "You saved me
from that hungry cat!"

"If it wasn't for you, Pitter,"
Tuffy told her, "I would still
be lost in the woods."

The three friends
looked at the
riverbank around
them. There were
sunbathing stones
for Tuffy,
tall grass for Pitter,
and lily pads for Polly.

"This place is perfect,"
Tuffy said.
"Yep," Pitter agreed.
"Sure is," said Polly.

The riverbank was quiet.

"But something's missing,"
Tuffy said.
"Yep," Pitter agreed.
"Sure is," said Polly.

Tuffy suddenly missed his
brothers and sisters. I didn't
say goodbye before I left,
he thought.
Tuffy felt homesick.

Pitter saw the tall grass and
wondered how she would
survive when winter came.
I don't know how to make a
nest, she thought.
Pitter felt quite foolish.

Polly realized that having
a tail was really wonderful.
She wanted to tell her brave
fish story to the other frogs.
Polly felt very proud.

"I miss home,"
Tuffy said.

"Yep," Pitter agreed.

"Me too," said Polly.

As the sky became dark, the
three little friends prepared for
sleep.

"Tomorrow morning,"
Pitter said,
"let's begin a new adventure...
across the river again,
through the forest,
and back to our homes...
where we belong."

"I agree," Tuffy yawned.
"We have a great story to tell
when we get back."
The three slept soundly on the riverbank
that night, tired from their long journey.

As the moonlight sparkled
across lily pads, Polly peeped
a little frog song to sing
her new friends to sleep:

"On the other side
The grass was greener,
But the peace they found
Inside was sweeter."

www.ingramcontent.com/pod-product-compliance
Lightning Source LLC
Chambersburg PA
CBHW040317100426
42811CB00012B/1466